She is healing

Theresa Lane

She is healing © 2022 Theresa Lane

All rights reserved.

No part of this publication may be reproduced, stored in a retrieval system, or transmitted, in any form or by any means, electronic, mechanical, photocopying, recording or otherwise, without the prior written permission of the presenters.

Theresa Lane asserts the moral right to be identified as author of this work.

Presentation by *BookLeaf Publishing*

Web: www.bookleafpub.com

E-mail: info@bookleafpub.com

ISBN: 9789357213790

First edition 2022

This book is for anyone and everyone.

Anyone healing, transforming and growing.

Anyone facing life's many trials and tribulations.

Anyone who wants to do better.

Anyone who knows deep down, they are capable of sooo much more.

Keep going.

I got this.

You got this.

WE GOT THIS.

i feel

i feel all the love
i feel all the pain
i feel all the sun
i feel all the rain

how can i explain
i am going insane
things just ain't the same
feeing numb in my brain

i can feel the change
up and down in my range
how can i explain
i am really not the same

i feel i feel i feel i feel
i feel love
i feel scared
i feel very unprepared
i feel fear
i feel light
i feel wrong
i feel right

what am i supposed to do?
i am feeling out of the blue
i really ain't got a clue
tell me how about you

i feel everything
every joy
every sting
this is my heart opening
cracking open
let it spring

stay present

present
i find myself escaping you
i have been escaping you for a really long time
through outside influences
or my own inner influences
of my own mind
or my body
or these feelings
struggles with the past
sadness in my heart
future anxieties
this mind had too many entities
who made it be like this
when will it stop
when will my mind, body and spirit become
besties full stop.

they are all screaming out for
presence.
here and now.

hate

i've absolutely hated myself
for a really long time
like really really hate

so much
i hated everything about me
my nose
my face
my hair
my legs
my teeth
my skin
my lips
my body
my reality
my life

everything on my body i hated
i even hated my name
wtf

now here i am
evolving
becoming aware
awakening to love

healing
connecting to mother earth
feeling all my emotions
good bad ugly

but what do i do with all this hate

deep issues
not yet resolved
and they have been coming up
they have had a home in my being
feels like for eons

the darkness
the pain
the anger
the shame
the doubt
the grief
all these have lived in my lane
the resentment
the jealousy
the hate
the pride
the fear
the lies
i find comfort in denial

oh why

i'm tired

so much to think about
so much to say
how can I make these thoughts go away
i'm tired of fighting
i'm tired of the war
can I just sit here
and be in love galore

no more fighting
no more victimising
i don't exist anywhere but now
yesterday's gone
tomorrow has yet to come

i know you are tired
so come back to here and now

anger

anger boils inside me
with the steam rising
up to hit my throat
transforming into the
most hateful words
you will ever hear

i curse you
i curse me
you curse you
you curse me
we go on and on
we may kick and scream

anger anger anger anger
i used to think only my dad had
these anger problems
but no,
mum had it too
she would suppress it
or take it out on me

anger
repressed anger
suppressed anger

it's all anger
we all feel anger
we all have anger

it's only now that
i am healing
i realise that it's collective

i can feel my mother's anger
my father's anger
my grandmother's anger
my grandfather's anger

then there is me
feeling alllll of this anger
that anyone around me
falls victim, they are in danger

it goes way back
it's pain in general
it's overwhelming
generational pain

here is beautiful

sometimes i get so sick of this artificial world
that we have created
i just wanna get out of 'here'
then i remember
i am expressing
in this time and space
as this, perfectly imperfect human
a child of the universe
beloved creature of love
and this is my home
my body
i cannot live without any of the elements

water air fire earth
earth air water fire
fire earth water air
elements elements
breathe through my hair

and it is beautiful here
it is our minds
and it's selfish desires
that have a conditioned reality
causing destruction and suffering

but here is beautiful
here is peace
here is nice
here is green
and all the colours of the rainbow
here is love
here is life
and i am here

i'm sorry

mother, mother
i'm so sorry
i forgot you
i'm so sorry i forgot you
mother, mother
i cry for you
i'm so sorry
that i tried to forget you
i long for you
oh how i long for you

i didn't want to remember you
because the pain hurt that bad
trust gone
heart broken shattered smashed
destroyed

what i had to endure before, after and during
your death
made me an angry damaged child
I masked the pain well
what a talented Gemini

thinking of you
now

yeah i feel beautiful
thinking of your love
yeah i feel mystical
and magical
extremely madly spiritual

i miss you so much
and to have you in my heart
means everything

but i get kinda scared a lot
doubt a lot
mad a lot

2022 be back to back with these triggers
i tried burying this pain
didn't think it'll all come back like this
again

because
i believed you were dead
i believed you were nothing
i hated this universe so much
i hated you so much
for leaving me here
i suffered so much
did you even care

real

who i am today
is who the younger me
always wanted to be
beautiful
wise
strong
confident

at times i slip off
and go back to my comfort zone
of being sad, ugly and lonely
but my foundation is being built
through all the pain, tears and agony
it's made me embrace myself even more
who really am i?
i'm still coming to know

self love
love this self
it took a long time to get here
and i still got a long way to go

(trust the journey
it's real)

crying

crying
all i can do is cry
and it is okay
these old feelings
ancient emotions
come up
in the present
and all i can do is cry
i have accepted that it is totally okay to cry
whenever
crying is purifying
it is releasing

i have to feel them
i feel them in my womb
and let my waters do what they gotta do
cry
it's beautiful

cry whenever you want okay
whenever you need to
it is sacred

i have been battling myself
there are parts of me don't wanna forgive

don't wanna face certain people i should face
blaming the world for all my hurt and pain

struggling to love myself
struggling to accept myself
can i just accept myself
i am so tired
i am so fucking tired
i am so fucking done with this bull shit
what are these thoughts that are so negative
bringing me down
do i have to keep enduring
why is it so dark
my emotions are full of pain
and full of blame
i cry
black butterfly
guide me
black butterfly
with the white spots
come back and visit me
come fly by me again
you remind me
that we all go through change
and its okay

we all eventually go from
caterpillar to butterfly

toxic

i'm jealous
i hate you
how dare you
fuck you
i love you
you're a piece of shit
son of a bitch
fuck you
i need you
i adore you
i hate you
fuck you
i love you

inner child wounds

i hate it here
i don't like it here
i don't like it here
no one understands me
no one understands me
my _____ calls me crazy
my _____ calls me dumb
my _____ calls me lazy
i take all these substances
they happily make me numb

i'm full of
unhealthy attachments
scheduled comparisons
deteriorating habits
no wonder i am foolish
no wonder i feel like shit
someone
take me out of here
i wanna go to the beach
or go to a river
ride on my bike
send whisky to my liver

love of my life

to the love of my life
thank you
thank you for loving this broken girl
you ignited a love inside me that i didn't even
know existed

i wrote to my diary
asking for a man like you
exactly like you
kind, beautiful, strong, understanding, loving
and caring
someone i can laugh with
fall in love with
stay in love with
joke with
take heaps of drugs with
be crazy with
avoid all my problems with
go on adventures with
eventually start a family with

who will love me so much
with a love so deep
that the ocean would be jealous

falling in love with you was the most beautiful
and also heart breaking thing at the same time
i am thankful
the universe delivered above and beyond for me

please know i will forever love you
please forgive me when my actions or choice of
words do not show it
i'm not perfect
you're not perfect

i love loving you
i love that you are for me
and that i am for you

if i died tomorrow

if i died tomorrow
i would be sad
because i didn't get to do what i really wanted in
this life

which is

1. express myself. like my most authentic self
2. be myself
3. not give a fuck
4. tell ALL the people i love that i love them
5. sing my songs
6. dance everyday
7. talk my shit freely - written and verbal.
wisdom & bullshit. my teachings & philosophies
8. pray with my friends and family
9. practice more gratitude
10. house a baby or two at the same time in my
womb. love them with all of my being
11. see the other side of generational trauma: a
healed nation

there's a part 2 to this somewhere

love that once

love that once fulfilled me
love that once made me the happiest
love that once excited me
love that once cherished me
love that once nourished me
love that once cradled me
love that once completed me
love that once carried me
love that once treasured me

it's falling away
and i can see
it's moving downhill
and i'm watching it
i'm standing back
watching it fall down
watching it crash
flames up in smoke
tears flow
so i can grow
the light inside me needs to glow
growing pains
oh i know
glowing stains
part of the show

my heart is awakening

my heart is awakening
i can feel it shakening
i can feel it palpitating
i can feel it re-elevating
alchemiser in my heart
i don't tell no lies
i feel a divine energy in me
you can see it in my eyes
heart heart open up open up

i need you
i feel you
you ease me
you please me
you feed me
feed me in your love
save me in your grace
love up on my mind
play up on my face

(feel your heart filling up with light
white light
and let it radiate across your being
breathe in
breathe out
repeat as necessary)

low times

always on my phone
wasting life away
my child self didn't even have a phone
she lived more free
she didn't take drugs
or eat fast food a lot
she played outside
everyday
she sung
she played games
she laughed
she climbed trees
ate flowers
rode bikes everyday
played with her street friends
wrote songs
read books
she was lovely

now i am older
i've developed these habits
so dependent on external
to give me satisfaction
and validation
so addicted

so attached
and so is everyone else
how can i break out of these habits

the fact that

the fact that i was created
the fact that i was thought of
the fact that..
the fact that i can even spit these words out
the fact that i can say the word 'fact'

roses are red
violets are blue
i was created by the same mysterious force
that created you

fear

fear makes me feel....

unworthy of myself
not good enough
scared of what people will say about me
replays the past of how others have hurt me
replays the memories of others doubting me
fear makes me hide away and never want to
come out
fear makes me dim my light all the way out
scared of everything
scared and worried
scared of judgement
scared of how i'm going to be seen
scared of what other people will say or think of
me
scared of being rejected
called names, being mocked for looking how i
look
acting how i act
fear is low and it makes me feel low
fear is negative
i fucking feel it
i feel it
i know

forgiveness

i am really out here learning how to live thru my
heart
i am really out here doing it
it's a lot of work!
reversing the voice of judgement, guilt, fear,
anger, hatred and infusing it with love
letting the love come in thru acceptance,
forgiveness and compassion
i haven't been taught this way

forgiveness
to forgive
i thought forgiveness was a one time thing,
that if i consciously chose to forgive someone
then thats it
fuck, i was wrong

i've learnt that u gotta forgive over and over and
over again
when the memory, the thought, the pain comes
back up
i forgive over and over again
for in the deep layer of the ocean in my self
i held on to the darkest of the darkest
literally lost inside me

but in that space
i found a deep need for pure unconditional love
that could only be filled with the power of
forgiveness
and who could so do that?

me

this is an "I' job
not for anyone else
but me
and so i forgive
as hard as it is, forgive
forgive with all the tears streaming down my
face
forgive while i'm screaming out to the skies
above
forgive with the essence of my whole entire
being aching

aching because its releasing the darkness its held
on to for so fucking long
forgive with the power of my breath
forgive, knowing it is the God within me that I
have finally found
that has led me to even forgive
to even be here, transforming myself
forgiving that perception
that has kept me enslaved

this has been my own suffering

judging or hating others and myself
never made me feel free or at peace
keep choosing love over
and over again
this is how i become free

heal thy self
heal the world

you got this

shine my love
you're a star
you got bars
you don't need nice cars

today i am under the sun
today i am having fun
today i pray like a nun
today i connect with my mum

shine my love
you were made to shine
you were made divine
brighter than the brightest light

i love you
i thank you
i forgive you

i am woman

strong brave woman
fiery spirit
warrior soul
healing light
enchanting glow
feminine energy
passionate light
divine supreme magic
we know the brightest light
the same way we know
the darkest night
power so strong
no energy comes close
to the power of the woman
the female
the creator of life
mother of mothers
her womb is full of magic
her womb holds all the answers
love the woman
love the womb-man

www.ingramcontent.com/pod-product-compliance
Lightning Source LLC
LaVergne TN
LVHW021333200726

843509LV00014B/2514